PLAYALONG 20/20
CLARINET
20 EASY POP HITS

Contact Us:
Hal Leonard
7777 West Bluemound Road
Milwaukee, WI 53213
Email: info@halleonard.com

In Europe contact:
Hal Leonard Europe Limited
Distribution Centre, Newmarket Road
Bury St Edmunds, Suffolk, IP33 3YB
Email: info@halleonardeurope.com

In Australia contact:
Hal Leonard Australia Pty. Ltd.
4 Lentara Court
Cheltenham, Victoria, 3192 Australia
Email: info@halleonard.com.au

Order No. AM1010724
ISBN 978-1-78305-988-1

For all works contained herein:
Unauthorized copying, arranging, adapting,
recording, internet posting, public performance,
or other distribution of the music in this
publication is an infringement of copyright.
Infringers are liable under the law.

Visit Hal Leonard Online at
www.halleonard.com

Arrangements by Christopher Hussey.
Backing tracks by Jeremy Birchall & Christopher Hussey.
Clarinet played by Howard McGill.
Audio recorded, mixed and mastered by
Jonas Persson & Imogen Hall.
Printed in the EU.

To acces audio visit:
www.halleonard.com/mylibrary
Enter Code:

6781-8505-6226-8985

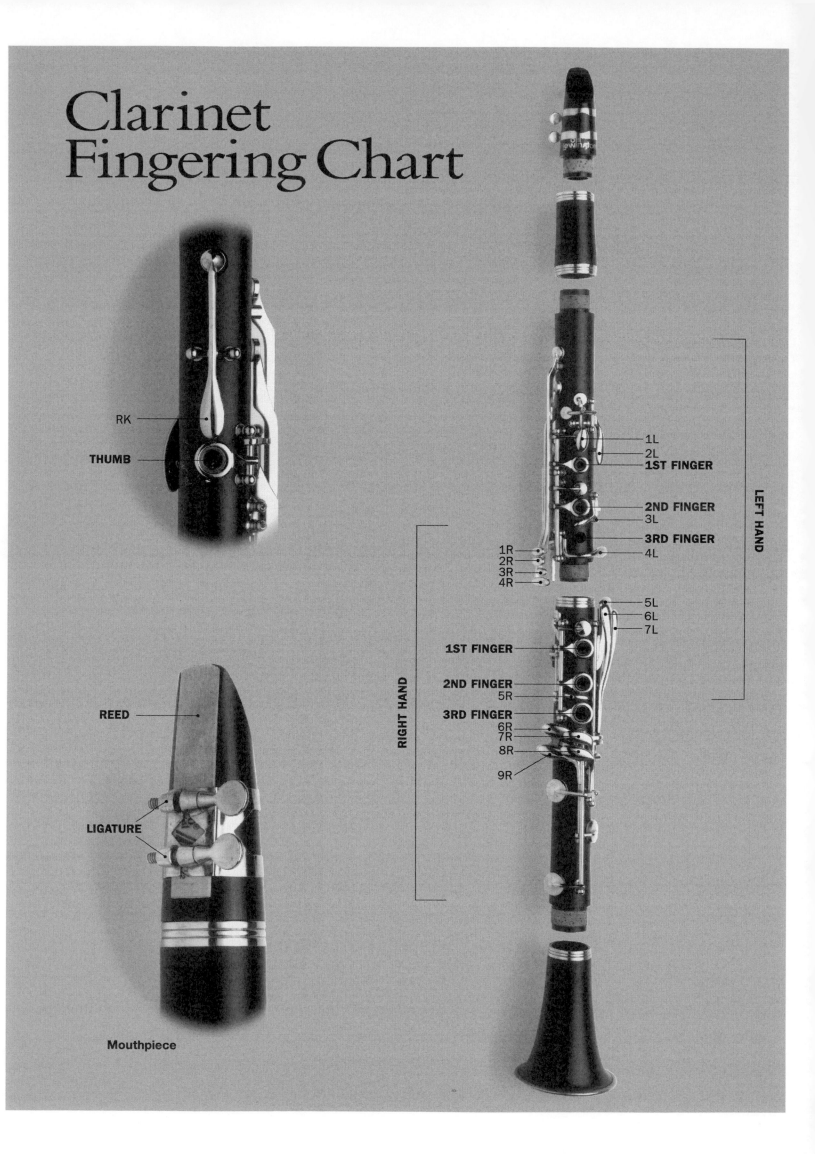

Clarinet Fingering Chart

RK

THUMB

REED

LIGATURE

Mouthpiece

1L
2L
1ST FINGER

2ND FINGER
3L

3RD FINGER
4L

1R
2R
3R
4R

5L
6L
7L

1ST FINGER

2ND FINGER
5R

3RD FINGER
6R
7R
8R

9R

LEFT HAND

RIGHT HAND

Indicates the lower limit of the best playing range for E♭, B♭, E♭ Alto and B♭ Bass Clarinets

Indicates the upper limit of the best playing range for E♭ and B♭ Clarinets

Indicates the upper limit of the best playing range for E♭ Alto and B♭ Bass Clarinets

Let It Go (from *Frozen*)

Words & Music by Kirsten Anderson-Lopez and Robert Lopez

Expressively ♩ = 68

© Copyright 2013 Wonderland Music Company Incorporated, USA.
All Rights Reserved. International Copyright Secured.

22 (Taylor Swift)

Words & Music by Taylor Swift, Max Martin & Johan Schuster

Lightly and excitedly ♩ = 104

© Copyright 2012 Taylor Swift Music/Sony/ATV Tree Publishing/MXM Music AB, Sweden.
Sony/ATV Music Publishing/Kobalt Music Publishing Limited.
All Rights Reserved. International Copyright Secured.

to Coda ⊕

D.S. al Coda

⊕ **Coda**

All Of Me (John Legend)

Words & Music by John Stephens and Toby Gad

Passionately ♩ = 126

(piano cue)

© Copyright 2013 John Legend Publishing and Gad Songs, LLC.
All Rights for John Legend Publishing Administered by BMG Rights Management (US) LLC.
All Rights for Gad Songs, LLC Administered by Atlas Music Group.
All Rights Reserved. Used by Permission.

34

mf

38

mp

42

mf

to Coda ⊕

46

mp

51

f

55

D.S. al Coda   ⊕ Coda

60

mp

64

mf

68

mp   *p*

Atlas (from *The Hunger Games: Catching Fire*)

Words & Music by Guy Berryman, Jonathan Buckland, William Champion & Christopher Martin

Melancholically ♩ = 137

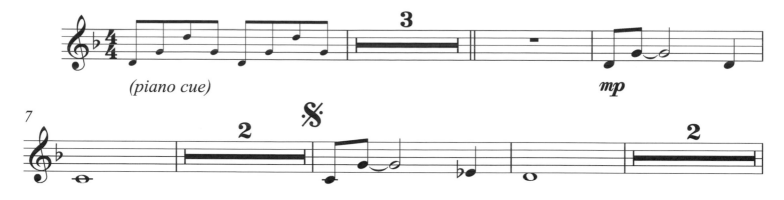

(piano cue)

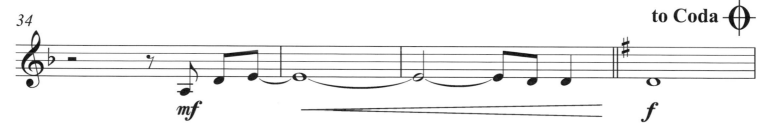

to Coda

D.S. al Coda

© Copyright 2013 Universal Music Publishing MGB Limited.
All Rights Reserved. International Copyright Secured.

Coda

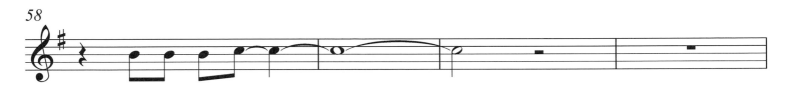

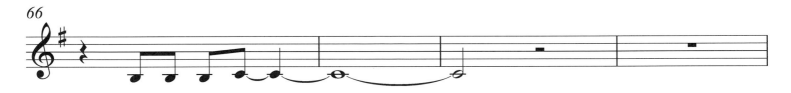

Best Song Ever (One Direction)

Words & Music by Wayne Hector, John Ryan, Julian Bunetta & Edward Drewett

Energetically ♩ = 118

(+ piano)

mf

13

17

20

f

23

27

31

35

mp

© Copyright 2013 BMG Platinum Songs US/Holy Cannoli Music/Music Of Big Deal/Bob Erotik Music/The Family Songbook.
Universal/MCA Music Limited/Warner/Chappell Music Publishing Limited/BMG Rights Management (US) LLC.
All Rights Reserved. International Copyright Secured.

Jar Of Hearts (Christina Perri)

Words & Music by Christina Perri, Drew Lawrence & Barrett Yeretsian

© Copyright 2010 WB Music Corp/Miss Perri Lane Publishing/Primary Wave Yeretsian/Piggy Dog Music.
Copyright Control/Fintage Publishing. B.V./Warner/Chappell North America Limited /BMG Rights Management (UK) Limited (Primary Wave).
All Rights Reserved. International Copyright Secured.

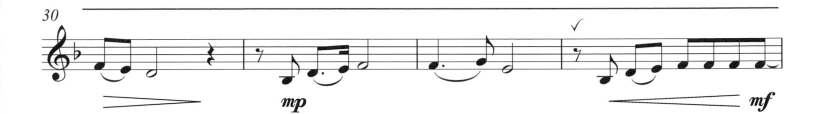

D.S. al Coda   **Coda**

molto rit.

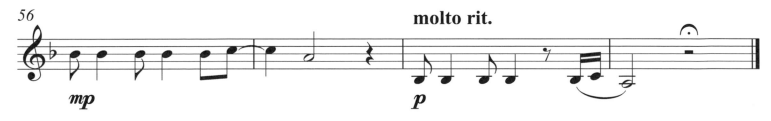

Just Give Me A Reason (Pink)

Words & Music by Alecia Moore, Jeff Bhasker & Nate Ruess

© Copyright 2012 Sony/ATV Songs LLC/Pink Inside Publishing/Way Above Music/W B Music Corp/EMI Blackwood Music Inc/FBR Music/Bearvon Music.
EMI Music Publishing Limited/Sony/ATV Music Publishing/Warner/Chappell North America Limited.
All Rights Reserved. International Copyright Secured.

Last Friday Night (Katy Perry)

Words & Music by Max Martin, Lukasz Gottwald, Bonnie McKee & Katy Perry

Confidently ♩ = 126

© Copyright 2010 Kasz Money Publishing/Maratone AB, Sweden/When I'm Rich You'll Be My Bitch, USA/Where Da Kasz At, USA/Prescription Songs LLC, USA/Bonnie McKee Music, USA.
Kobalt Music Publishing Limited/Warner/Chappell North America Limited/Downtown Music Publishing LLC.
All Rights Reserved. International Copyright Secured.

to Coda ⊕

1.

mf

2.   *(sax solo)*   **D.S. al Coda**

f

⊕ **Coda**

mf

Make You Feel My Love (Adele)

Words & Music by Bob Dylan

© Copyright 1997 Special Rider Music, USA.
Music Sales Corporation (ASCAP).
All Rights Reserved. International Copyright Secured.

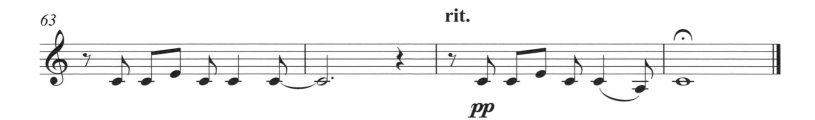

Once Upon A Dream (from *Maleficent*)

Words & Music by Sammy Fain & Jack Lawrence

© Copyright 1952 Walt Disney Music Company, USA.
All Rights Reserved. International Copyright Secured.

Panic Cord (Gabrielle Aplin)

Words & Music by Jez Ashurst, Gabrielle Aplin & Nicholas Atkinson

Steadily, with a bounce ♩ = 106

(synth. vocals cue)

© Copyright 2013 Major 3rd Music Limited.
Universal Music Publishing Limited/BMG Rights Management (UK) Limited/Stage Three Music Publishing Limited.
All Rights Reserved. International Copyright Secured.

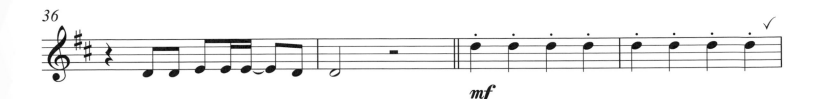

Right Place Right Time (Olly Murs)

Words & Music by Stephen Robson, Claude Kelly & Oliver Murs

© Copyright 2013 Studio Beast Music/Salli Isaak Music Publishing Limited/Imagem CV/Warner-Tamerlane Publishing Co.
Universal Music Publishing Limited/Imagem Music/Warner/Chappell North America Limited.
All Rights Reserved. International Copyright Secured.

f legato

D.S. al Coda

Coda

mf

f

mf

Say Something (A Great Big World, feat. Christina Aguilera)

Words & Music by Mike Campbell, Chad Vaccarino & Ian Axel

© Copyright 2011 Songs Of Universal Incorporated/Chad Vaccarino Publishing/Ian Axel Music /Songtrust Blvd.
Universal/MCA Music Limited/ST Music LLC.
All Rights Reserved. International Copyright Secured.

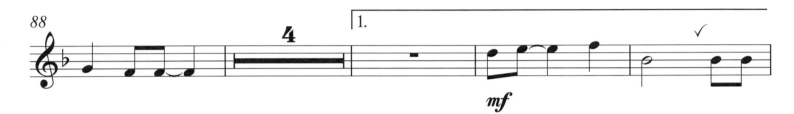

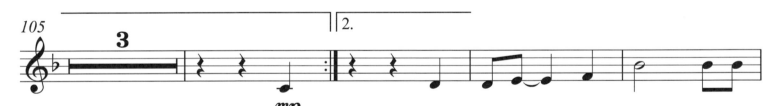

A Sky Full Of Stars (Coldplay)

Words & Music by Guy Berryman, Jonathan Buckland, William Champion, Christopher Martin & Tim Bergling

Smoothly ♩ = 124

© Copyright 2014 Universal Music Publishing MGB Limited/EMI Music Publishing Ltd.
All Rights Reserved. International Copyright Secured.

to Coda ⊕

D.S. al Coda

12

(+ drums)

⊕ **Coda**

f

(Instrumental)

16

8

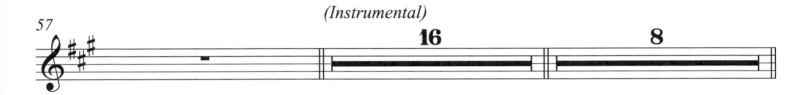

f

7

mf

mp

33

Stay (Rihanna, feat. Mikky Ekko)

Words & Music by Justin Parker & Mikky Ekko

Tenderly ♩ = 112

© Copyright 2012 Sony ATV Tunes LLC/Kkids And Stray Dogs.
Sony/ATV Music Publishing.
All Rights Reserved. International Copyright Secured.

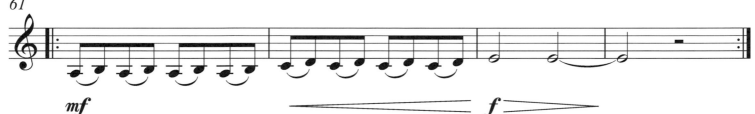

Titanium (David Guetta)

Words & Music by Sia Furler, David Guetta, Giorgio Tuinfort & Nick van de Wall

Energetically ♩ = 126

© Copyright 2011 Piano Songs/Afrojack Publishing.
EMI Music Publishing Limited/BMG Rights Management (UK) Limited/What A Publishing Limited.
All Rights Reserved. International Copyright Secured.

38

42

f

mf

f

(2nd time cresc.)

2.

5

f

What Makes You Beautiful (One Direction)

Words & Music by Savan Kotecha, Carl Falk & Rami Yacoub

Steadily and smoothly ♩ = 125

© Copyright 2011 Oh Suki Music/EMI April Music Inc./Rami Productions AB/BMG Chrysalis Scandinavia AB, Sweden/Kobalt Music Copyrights SARL.
Chrysalis Music Limited/EMI Music Publishing Limited /Kobalt Music Publishing Limited.
All Rights Reserved. International Copyright Secured.

28

31

to Coda ⊕

35

1.　　　　　　　　　2.

mf　　　　　　*mf*

39

44

mp

47

50

D.S. al Coda

f

⊕ Coda

53

Wrecking Ball (Miley Cyrus)

Words & Music by Stephan Moccio, Sacha Skarbek, Lukasz Gottwald, Henry Russell Walter & Maureen McDonald

© Copyright 2013 Sing Little Penguin/Kasz Money Publishing/Prescription Songs/Songs Of Universal Inc/Oneirology Publishing/EMI April Music Inc/BMG Rights Management GMBH/Mo Zella Mo Music.
Kobalt Music Publishing Limited/Universal/MCA Music Limited/BMG Rights Management (UK) Limited/EMI Music Publishing Limited.
All Rights Reserved. International Copyright Secured.

to Coda ⊕

D.S. al Coda

⊕ **Coda**

Someone Like You (Adele)

Words & Music by Daniel Wilson & Adele Adkins

Smoothly, with tenderness ♩ = 68

mp espressivo

poco cresc.

mp   *mf*

© Copyright 2010 Sugar Lake Music LLC/Melted Stone Publishing Limited.
Chrysalis Music Limited/Universal Music Publishing Limited.
All Rights Reserved. International Copyright Secured.

23

26

f

mf

28

mp

31

mp

35

38

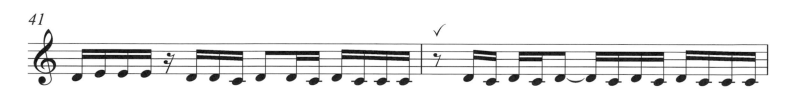

mf

41

43

mp

poco rit.

A tempo

1.　　　　2.

Skyfall (from *Skyfall*)

Words & Music by Adele Adkins & Paul Epworth

© Copyright 2012 EMI Music Publishing Ltd. and Melted Stone Publishing Ltd/Universal Music Publishing Limited.
All Rights for EMI Music Publishing Ltd. in the U.S. and Canada Controlled and Administered by EMI April Music Inc.
All Rights Reserved. International Copyright Secured. Used by Permission.

(brass cue)

46

62

65

f

68

ff

71

74

78

f

molto rit.

81

85 Freely

(guitar)   *mp*   *(brass/strings)*   *p*